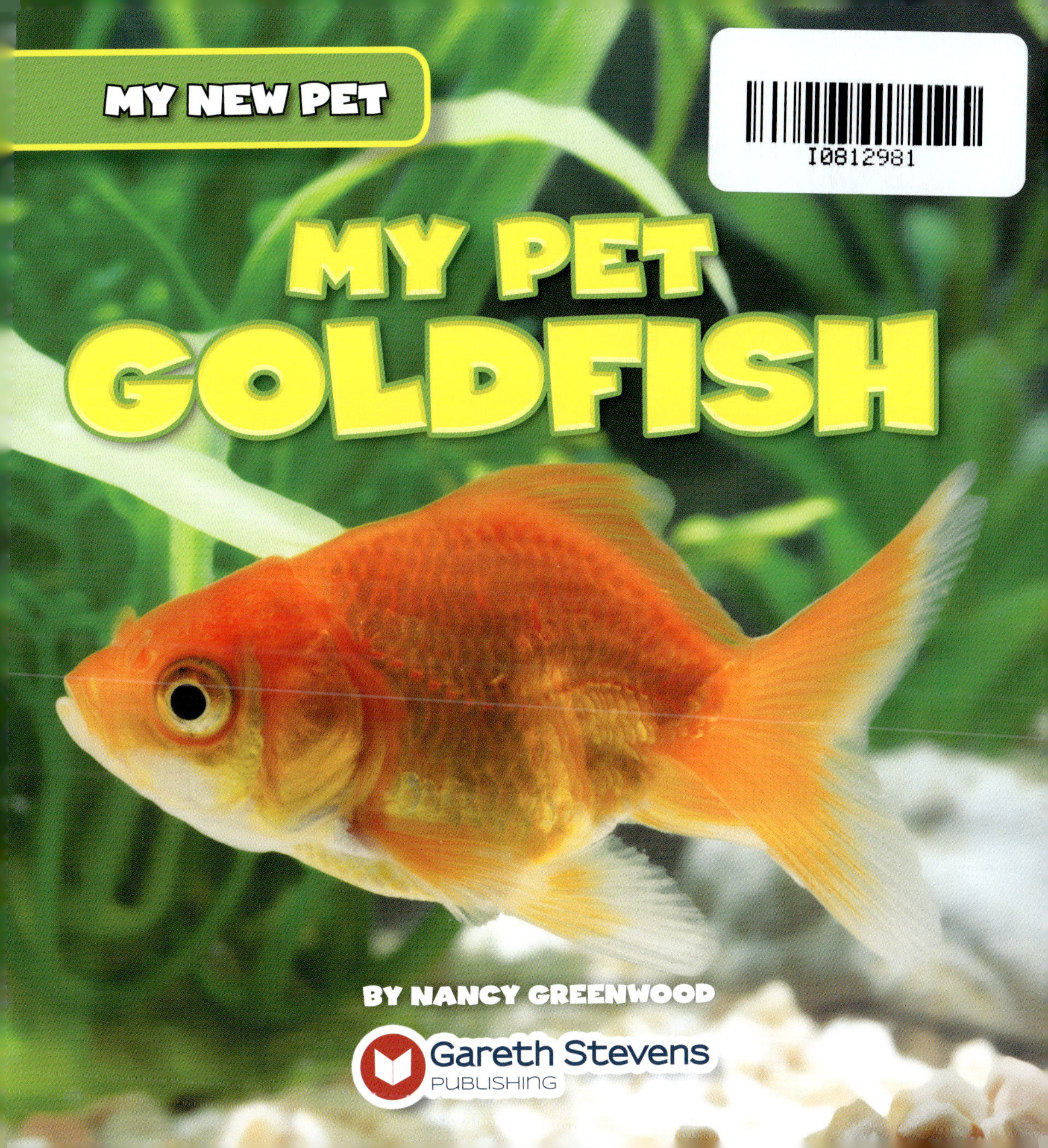

MY NEW PET

MY PET GOLDFISH

BY NANCY GREENWOOD

Gareth Stevens PUBLISHING

Please visit our website, www.garethstevens.com. For a free color catalog of all our high-quality books, call toll free 1-800-542-2595 or fax 1-877-542-2596.

Portions of this work were originally authored by Cecelia H. Brannon and published as *Pet Goldfish*. All new material this edition authored by Nancy Greenwood.

Library of Congress Cataloging-in-Publication Data
Names: Greenwood, Nancy, author.
Title: My pet goldfish / Nancy Greenwood.
Description: New York : Gareth Stevens Publishing, [2023] | Series: My new pet | Includes index.
Identifiers: LCCN 2021061240 | ISBN 9781538281000 (set) | ISBN 9781538281017 (library binding) | ISBN 9781538280997 (paperback) | ISBN 9781538281024 (ebook)
Subjects: LCSH: Goldfish–Juvenile literature.
Classification: LCC SF458.G6 G74 2023 | DDC 639.3/7484–dc23/eng/20220111
LC record available at https://lccn.loc.gov/2021061240

Published in 2023 by
Gareth Stevens Publishing
29 East 21st Street
New York, NY 10010

Designer: Andrea Davison-Bartolotta
Editor: Kristen Nelson

Photo credits: Cover, p.1 Tony Stock/Shutterstock.com; series art (interior backgrounds) Magnia/Shutterstock.com; p. 5 Dikushin Dmitry/Shutterstock.com; p. 7 luckypic/Shutterstock.com; p. 9 New Africa/Shutterstock.com; p. 11 pritsana/Shutterstock.com; p. 13 Ja Crispy/Shutterstock.com; p. 15 Vixtor Photo/Shutterstock.com; p. 17 Mirek Kijewski/Shutterstock.com; p. 19 SpeedKingz/Shutterstock.com;CCISUL/Shutterstock.com .

Printed in the United States of America

CPSIA compliance information: Batch #CSGS23: For further information contact Gareth Stevens, New York, New York at 1-800-542-2595.

CONTENTS

Boldface words appear in the glossary.

Your Pet Goldfish

Do you want a pet? If you've never had one before, a goldfish can be a good first pet. Having any pet is big a **responsibility**, but goldfish are fairly easy to care for. Goldfish can live alone or many can live in one **tank**.

About Goldfish

Most goldfish are yellow or orange. Some have black or white **scales** too. A goldfish has seven fins. These help it swim all over its tank. You can put **decorations** in your fish's tank. Your fish may go inside one.

Lots of Water

The most important thing goldfish need to live is water. They should live in a bowl or tank filled with water. The tank should be large so that the goldfish has room to swim around and grow.

Your fish's water needs to be clean. The bowl or tank should be cleaned every week. The goldfish must be out of the bowl before you clean it. Use a special **net** to move it to another bowl with water. An adult can help.

Feeding Your Fish

Goldfish need to be fed at least once a day. They eat fish food. This is commonly in the form of flakes. You should **sprinkle** the flakes on top of the water. You can buy fish food at a pet store.

The Life of a Goldfish

Goldfish can be different sizes. Some can grow to be longer than this book, although it's not common. If you take good care of your goldfish, it could live 30 years! Most goldfish don't live that long however.

Goldfish don't sleep the same way people do. A goldfish keeps its eyes open when it sleeps. This is because goldfish don't have **eyelids**. A goldfish commonly stays in one spot while sleeping, moving only a little to stay **upright**.

Getting a Goldfish

If you think a goldfish would be a good pet for you, ask an adult you live with about it. Goldfish may be fairly easy to care for, but they need clean water, food, and a nice space to swim.

Sometimes you can win goldfish as prizes at fairs. You can also buy them from pet stores. When you get your fish, it might be in a bag of water. You'll need to have a bowl or tank ready when your new pet comes home.

GLOSSARY

decorations: Something added to something else to make it look nice.

eyelids: Either of the two movable pieces of skin that cover some animals' eyes when closed.

net: A tool used for catching or holding things made of pieces of string, rope, or wire woven together with spaces in between.

responsibility: Something a person is in charge of.

scale: One of many small plates that cover the bodies of some animals, such as fish.

sprinkle: To put small pieces or amounts of something over something else.

tank: A container for holding or storing things.

upright: In a position to be straight up.

FOR MORE INFORMATION

BOOKS

Brainard, Jason. *Is a Fish a Good Pet for Me?* New York, NY: PowerKids Press, 2020.

Gagne, Tammy. *Caring for Fish: A 4D Book.* North Mankato, MN: Pebble, 2019.

Titmus, Dawn. *Fish.* New York, NY: PowerKids Press, 2019.

WEBSITES

Goldfish
www.ducksters.com/animals/goldfish.php
Find out more about these popular pet fish.

Pet Fish
www.dkfindout.com/us/animals-and-nature/pet-care/pet-fish/
Read more about goldfish and other pet fish on this interactive website.

Publisher's note to educators and parents: Our editors have carefully reviewed these websites to ensure that they are suitable for students. Many websites change frequently, however, and we cannot guarantee that a site's future contents will continue to meet our high standards of quality and educational value. Be advised that students should be closely supervised whenever they access the internet.

INDEX